Goodbye Tomorrow

Goodbye Tomorrow

Richard O. Ovuorho

authorHOUSE®

AuthorHouse™
1663 Liberty Drive
Bloomington, IN 47403
www.authorhouse.com
Phone: 1-800-839-8640

Published by AuthorHouse   11/20/2012

ISBN: 978-1-4772-3864-6 (sc)
ISBN: 978-1-4772-3866-0 (e)

Dedicated to my angel, Feli,
and Emma

Author's Note

This poem is in two parts. Part one is about relationships, while part two is about contemporary issues.

Brief Biodata

Richard O. Ovuorho is a practising engineer who has flare for literary works. He has published a theatrical piece, *Reaping The Whirlwind,* and a memoir, *My Grandfather*. He has many unpublished literary works. The prose *My Grandfather* was a finalist in the 2007 Association of Nigerian Authors (ANA) literary awards, in the category ANA/Chevron Prose Prize on Environmental Issues. *Goodbye Tomorrow* is his first published work of poetry.

He holds a master's degree of production engineering from the University of Benin, Benin City, Nigeria, and is currently working with The Shell Petroleum Development Company of Nigeria Limited as a senior facilities engineer. He is a native of Eku, in Ethiope-East Local Government Area of Delta state, Nigeria. He is married to Felicia and is blessed with Emmanuel.

Contents

Part One

Part Two

Part One

My African Bride

So beautiful, the blossomed rose,
like the moon, she glows in splendour,
radiating scintillating qualities,
which illuminate my universe
with her bright bold chocolate beauty.

Fleshy and juicy her body,
her legs walk elegance and grace.
With thrilling and exhilarating fingers,
her eyes dreamily and lovely,
her hands knitting industry.

Her appearance, alluring and captivating
with careful and respectful character,
her speech, a lullaby and encouragement
with the wisdom of biblical Solomon,
and laughter reigns with her presence.

A gorgeous and wonderfully crafted rib,
the curator of African tradition and beauty,
with sleek and shapely sculptured curves
as she exudes the sweet fragrance of true love,
with contentment, I hold her for eternity.

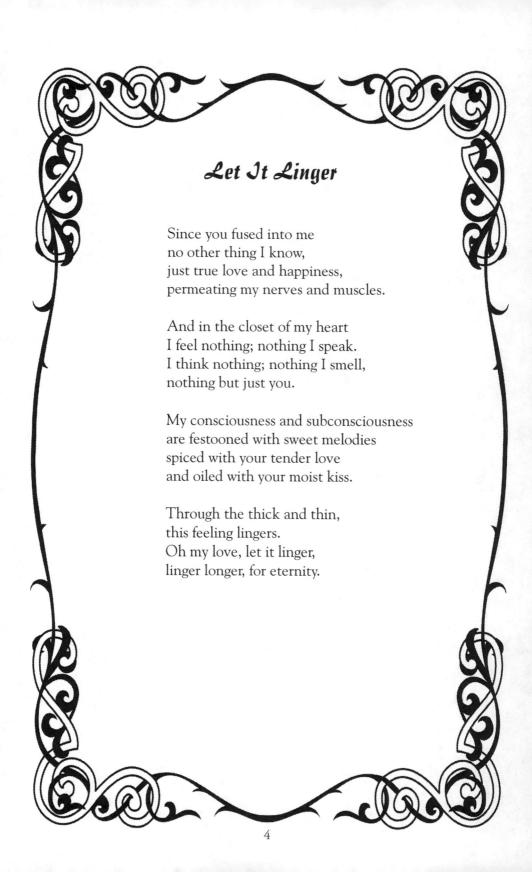

Let It Linger

Since you fused into me
no other thing I know,
just true love and happiness,
permeating my nerves and muscles.

And in the closet of my heart
I feel nothing; nothing I speak.
I think nothing; nothing I smell,
nothing but just you.

My consciousness and subconsciousness
are festooned with sweet melodies
spiced with your tender love
and oiled with your moist kiss.

Through the thick and thin,
this feeling lingers.
Oh my love, let it linger,
linger longer, for eternity.

Pendulum

There's the nectar, ripe, succulent, and appetizing,
and there's the insect, rugged but gentle like a lamb.
With wings flapping and hovering,
he dances around like a floater on rumbling stream,
in consonance with the drum beat,
drum beat by heavenly drummer.

The rhythm increases in tempo,
then gracefully dances the nectar
like the woofer of a loudspeaker.
And they cling as magnet and metal,
glued together by nature scented gum,
to propagate the bond of love.

The drum beat increases in crescendo
and sensual vibrations reverberate.
The wings flutter and the bodies quiver,
as the dispersants spread
cemented, to part not asunder,
from generation to generation, cyclical.

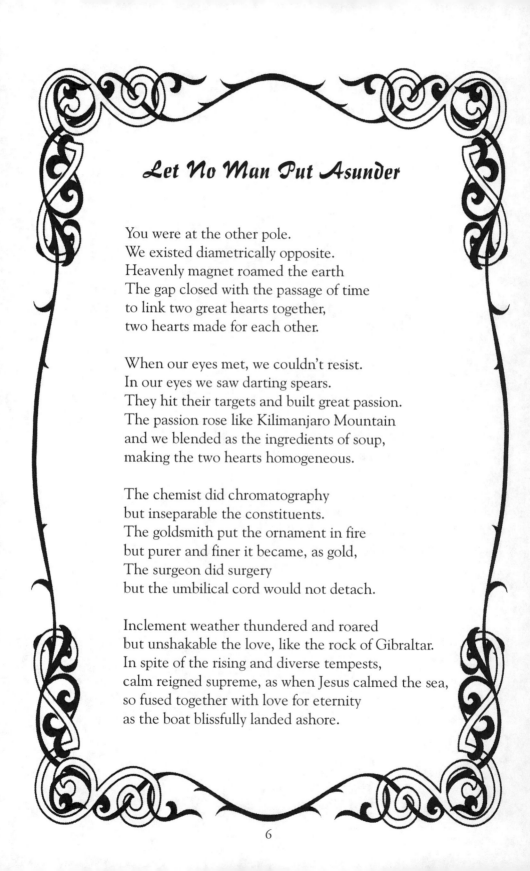

Let No Man Put Asunder

You were at the other pole.
We existed diametrically opposite.
Heavenly magnet roamed the earth
The gap closed with the passage of time
to link two great hearts together,
two hearts made for each other.

When our eyes met, we couldn't resist.
In our eyes we saw darting spears.
They hit their targets and built great passion.
The passion rose like Kilimanjaro Mountain
and we blended as the ingredients of soup,
making the two hearts homogeneous.

The chemist did chromatography
but inseparable the constituents.
The goldsmith put the ornament in fire
but purer and finer it became, as gold,
The surgeon did surgery
but the umbilical cord would not detach.

Inclement weather thundered and roared
but unshakable the love, like the rock of Gibraltar.
In spite of the rising and diverse tempests,
calm reigned supreme, as when Jesus calmed the sea,
so fused together with love for eternity
as the boat blissfully landed ashore.

Skill for Ecstasy

Soccer is a game:
two teams to play
in mutual interaction
spiced with incisive movements,
dribbling with stylistic displays.
Everyone it thrills,
when skilfully played.

A trick by the midfielder,
the wall of defence is displaced
and the chance created
for the striker to shoot,
and score a goal, the climax,
the stadium agog
with resounding satisfaction.

The passion is soccer,
two teams to tangle
in mutual understanding.
Spiced with stylistic movements,
dribbling with stylistic tongues 'n' fingers,
everyone it thrills
When skilfully played.

A flick by the midfinger,
the walls of defence then displaced,
as the winger prods forward
for the striker to shoot,
and score an orgasmic goal.
The bodies quiver, then, tranquil,
smack with resounding satisfaction.

You Fill Me

Whenever I punch my keyboard,
your image fills my screen
to display your immeasurable beauties.

Whenever I open my drawer for a file,
your picture jumps out instead,
to fill my hands with blessings.

Whenever I read the dailies,
your story dots every page
craftily written without printer's devil.

Whenever I seat behind the wheel,
your tender hands I feel
to steer me home safely.

Whether in the deep and dark,
you alone I see and feel
to illuminate my life's path.

Whenever, wherever, whatever,
thinking of you is satisfaction
'Cause you fill me with contentment.

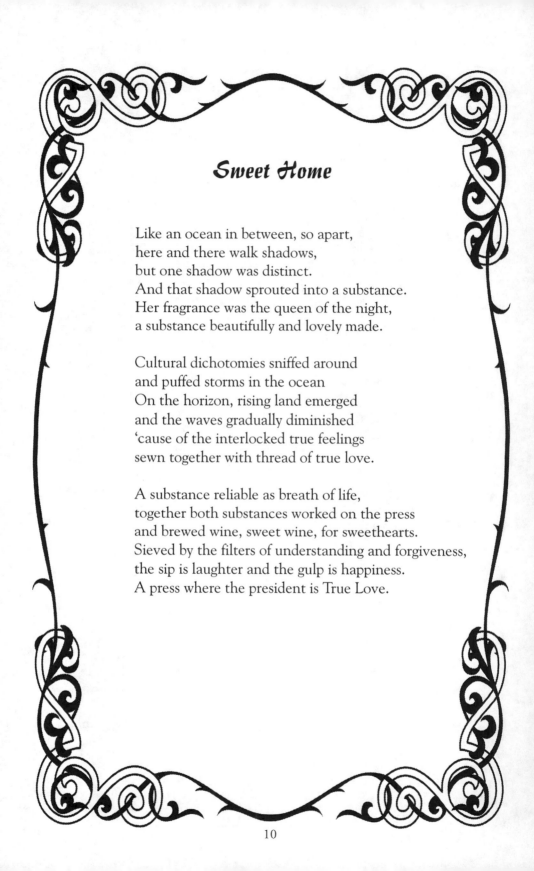

Sweet Home

Like an ocean in between, so apart,
here and there walk shadows,
but one shadow was distinct.
And that shadow sprouted into a substance.
Her fragrance was the queen of the night,
a substance beautifully and lovely made.

Cultural dichotomies sniffed around
and puffed storms in the ocean
On the horizon, rising land emerged
and the waves gradually diminished
'cause of the interlocked true feelings
sewn together with thread of true love.

A substance reliable as breath of life,
together both substances worked on the press
and brewed wine, sweet wine, for sweethearts.
Sieved by the filters of understanding and forgiveness,
the sip is laughter and the gulp is happiness.
A press where the president is True Love.

The Jolly Ride

Eye to eye, the beginning,
then the planting of seedlings
and a seed germinates,
nurturing and nurturing,
and a plant implants

Like a magnet attracts a metal,
so flung together
and interlocked as a web,
an inseparable union
as great a feeling as Mount Everest

And greatly given, unconditionally.
Groomed only by reciprocity,
cemented by live and let live,
like a locomotive fired by tons of coal,
so sustained by understanding and forgiveness

Like the nerves and neurones
so maintained by effective communication,
always there as one's breath
on a coast to coast marital voyage
till Transition calls.

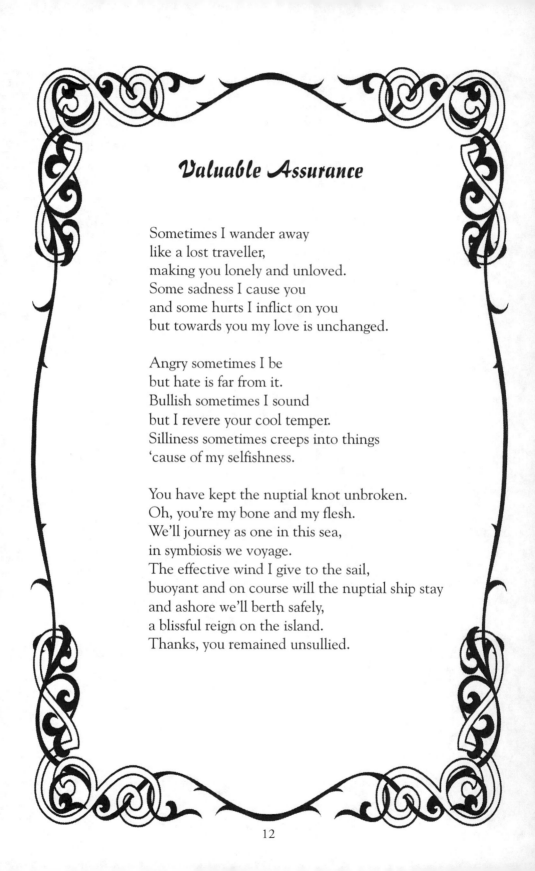

Valuable Assurance

Sometimes I wander away
like a lost traveller,
making you lonely and unloved.
Some sadness I cause you
and some hurts I inflict on you
but towards you my love is unchanged.

Angry sometimes I be
but hate is far from it.
Bullish sometimes I sound
but I revere your cool temper.
Silliness sometimes creeps into things
'cause of my selfishness.

You have kept the nuptial knot unbroken.
Oh, you're my bone and my flesh.
We'll journey as one in this sea,
in symbiosis we voyage.
The effective wind I give to the sail,
buoyant and on course will the nuptial ship stay
and ashore we'll berth safely,
a blissful reign on the island.
Thanks, you remained unsullied.

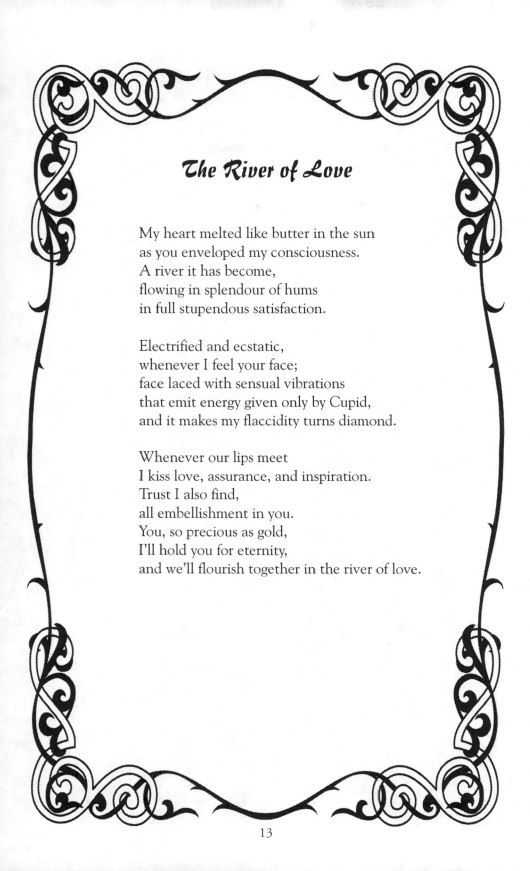

The River of Love

My heart melted like butter in the sun
as you enveloped my consciousness.
A river it has become,
flowing in splendour of hums
in full stupendous satisfaction.

Electrified and ecstatic,
whenever I feel your face;
face laced with sensual vibrations
that emit energy given only by Cupid,
and it makes my flaccidity turns diamond.

Whenever our lips meet
I kiss love, assurance, and inspiration.
Trust I also find,
all embellishment in you.
You, so precious as gold,
I'll hold you for eternity,
and we'll flourish together in the river of love.

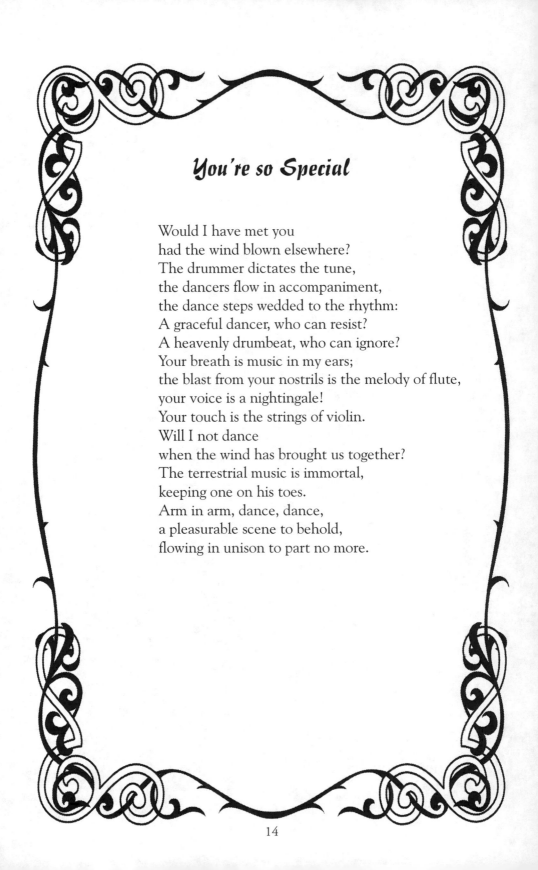

You're so Special

Would I have met you
had the wind blown elsewhere?
The drummer dictates the tune,
the dancers flow in accompaniment,
the dance steps wedded to the rhythm:
A graceful dancer, who can resist?
A heavenly drumbeat, who can ignore?
Your breath is music in my ears;
the blast from your nostrils is the melody of flute,
your voice is a nightingale!
Your touch is the strings of violin.
Will I not dance
when the wind has brought us together?
The terrestrial music is immortal,
keeping one on his toes.
Arm in arm, dance, dance,
a pleasurable scene to behold,
flowing in unison to part no more.

Tree by the River

True Love, True Love, where are you?
Here, by the river bank.

True Love, True Love, now I can see you.
Oh, you are welcome, my dear friend.

True Love, True Love, you're so healthy.
Yes, your observation is cute.

True Love, True Love, your leaves are so green.
Yes, because my roots are enmeshed in compost.

True Love, True Love, your fruits are fresh and succulent.
Yes, because I give the leaves what the roots absorb.

True Love, True Love, how come you are progressive?
I'm selfless and supportive.

True Love, True Love, what is the secret?
Oh, we live by nourishment, as one body.

True Love, True Love, what type of nourishment?
We are bonded as one, in the compost of love.

True Love, True Love, I envy your relationship.
Therefore do likewise with your neighbour.

True Love, True Love, I will just do that as I leave you.
And your relationship will thrive and peace reign.

The Ember of Love

In your eyes I see fire,
an unconsuming fire.
It fans the ember of love,
the love that's tender and kind,
which glows like a full moon

'Cause you're Love epitomised,
I send you this,
straight from the heart,
to let you know
that you're the love of my life.

Near but Far Away

Lo! There she is.
Can't you see her?
There! That rose in the rising sun,
fresh and succulent,
captivating but tantalising,
lovely but slippery

How close and near she is,
but how far and distant too.
The nearer I walk,
the farther she becomes,
vaporising like a mirage.

But why so elusive?
Come, touch me; feel me.
See how I'm tender and delicious
and aflame with passion.
Why so near but far away?

Promise Inverse

Into the stream of comfort you led me,
bathed me with the water of hope,
rubbed me with the cream of trust,
drenched me in happiness.
And into the sky we lifted like an airbus,
gaining altitude by the days
together as pilot and co-pilot
headed for the promised land.

The landing gears were ready
but you vaporised suddenly
and drove splintered glass into my heart,
a young heart set to love,
thus switching the radar of sadness for joy,
and you advertised me in ruin,
as devastated as a crashed airplane.
Excruciating pains and stresses now my companions,
none would I have experienced
had you not ask me to fly with you.

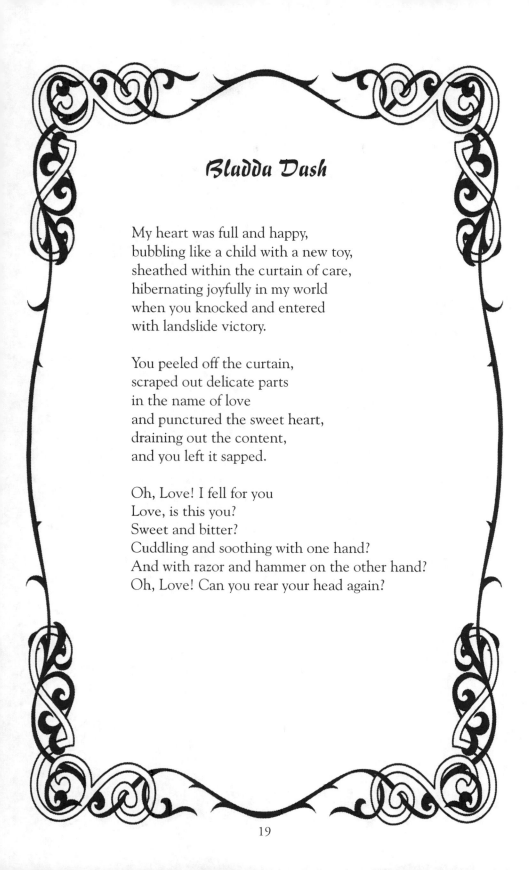

Bladda Dash

My heart was full and happy,
bubbling like a child with a new toy,
sheathed within the curtain of care,
hibernating joyfully in my world
when you knocked and entered
with landslide victory.

You peeled off the curtain,
scraped out delicate parts
in the name of love
and punctured the sweet heart,
draining out the content,
and you left it sapped.

Oh, Love! I fell for you
Love, is this you?
Sweet and bitter?
Cuddling and soothing with one hand?
And with razor and hammer on the other hand?
Oh, Love! Can you rear your head again?

Rhythmic Deceit

Let me whisper in your ears
the words of endearment!

Let me incite your feeling
with the caress of oneness.

Let me inundate you
with my millions of life.

Let me swim in you,
but I won't inflate your cocoon.

Oh, baby, now I feel eerie!
What? I promised? Go away with your swollen cocoon!

Irreversible

Every second and every minute
I expel sweet breeze
but coldness returns.
Where are you?

Every minute and every hour
I call and wait for your response,
but echoes upon echoes return.
Where are you?

Every hour and every day
I crane my neck to catch your glimpse
but opaque and obscure images float before me.
Where are you?

Every day and every week
I scour the Net for your email
but only sent mails I see.
Where are you?

Every week and every month
I wait for the postman for your letter
but the postman passes over me.
Where are you?

Every month and every year
I sink into abyss of loneliness
'cause coldness and boredom are my lone companions
Where are you?

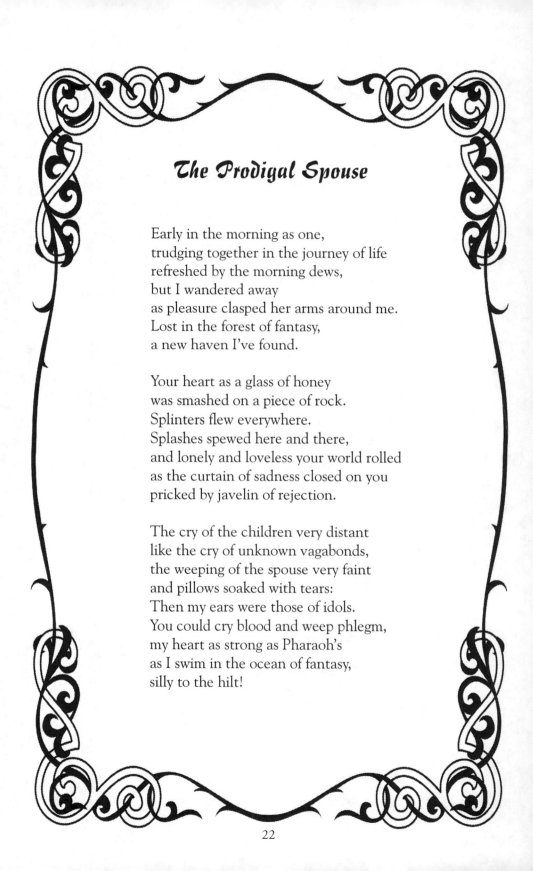

The Prodigal Spouse

Early in the morning as one,
trudging together in the journey of life
refreshed by the morning dews,
but I wandered away
as pleasure clasped her arms around me.
Lost in the forest of fantasy,
a new haven I've found.

Your heart as a glass of honey
was smashed on a piece of rock.
Splinters flew everywhere.
Splashes spewed here and there,
and lonely and loveless your world rolled
as the curtain of sadness closed on you
pricked by javelin of rejection.

The cry of the children very distant
like the cry of unknown vagabonds,
the weeping of the spouse very faint
and pillows soaked with tears:
Then my ears were those of idols.
You could cry blood and weep phlegm,
my heart as strong as Pharaoh's
as I swim in the ocean of fantasy,
silly to the hilt!

Suddenly the cloud lifted its curtains
and the midday sun scotched my skin.
The glittering diamond suddenly darkened
as pleasure's arms unclasped and slapped.
The pain reverberated like the ripples of water
and the forest of fantasy was hewn.
Realisation hit hard at my chin,
and dazed me awake.

Now long shadows dot the ground.
Where is the route?
Will tears still be flowing?
Will the misty eyes recognise me?
Will the sobbing and pained arms open?
The clutches of guilt are enormous,
but I'll journey with an olive branch.
Perhaps the olive oil will soothe the pains.

Missing You

The fire brigade team did some work
to put out the fire!
And the medics, too, battled,
but none could succeed,
'cause the fire was immense.
Only you can quench it.
I am missing you greatly.

Engraved in My Heart

'Cause I hold you so precious as gold,
I send you this
to let you know
I've carved you in my heart.

The strong bound of love,
though it didn't yield nuptial fruit,
will not make me love you less
'cause I've carved you in my heart.

My love for you only Cupid could tell,
but I wish you the very best
in your life journey,
though I've carved you in my heart.

Part Two

The Visitor

There she lurks, a prostitute on beat!
Smiling and friendly ' cause of the expectation,
arms welcomely yet insidiously spread,
with eyes blinking like an owl's.

She visits unawares,
at unwholesome time,
and unwelcomed, like an estranged lover,
yet she insists as the setting sun.

And when she breathes,
it's anguish and tears,
sorrows and weeping,
losses and devastation.

Go away! Go away!
Away from me, you beautiful ruin!
But she's adamant as a flowing stream
'cause she must rise as the morning sun.

Oh, come! Come!
For you're indispensable,
being common as the air,
but only when I'm spent.

The Elusive Romance

To serve and to protect the chick,
being friends in romance,
the hawk dressed in immaculate uniform,
cultured, nurtured, and groomed like a groom.

Distrust, as loose cotton before the wind, dispersed
justice and fairness astride nooks and cranny
and motorists now princes on every route
as extortion becomes footprint on a sandy shore.

Now the chicks are treated lovely
as bail, granted independence as the air.
Criminal investigation judiciously concluded
and accidental discharge committed to the gallows.

Now brutality swept away by tsunami
as procession and assembly walk the street
protected and guarded like kings,
human right abuses as dead as corpses.

The cry of Uhuru! Of love between the hawks and chicks!
But lamentation and weeping slap one awake,
and reality stands, hands akimbo, with misty eyes,
as the hawk just descended on the chick!

Homeless

Emptiness, just emptiness and loneliness!
The edifice turned a statue with masculine biceps
exhibiting insensitive muscles and uncaring nerves,
and mighty arms that embrace not.
Though it has bright eyes, it's blind as a bat.

A rich edifice, but loneliness reigns as a graveyard.
It desires fullness for attention; attention for fullness,
but the goat stands for the hen; he-goat for cock,
'cause they're out to scratch and peck,
the gathered grains never enough.

The chicks here and there, everywhere crèches.
Lacking fullness for attention and attention for fullness
so their growth and development bequeathed
to create Frankensteins most times,
and social immorality and destitute parade the street.

On the horizon, emptiness grows.
Who can bring twilight? When?
To give birth to a dawn of attention and fullness,
else the edifice is subsumed into abyss
and family morality and dignity vaporise like ether.

My Beloved Sweetheart

Oh, blessed! You're blessed with six-lettered name
'cause I endowed you in all ramifications,
even in the beginning.

Agrarian, your first name,
yet hunger clothes your offspring
'Cause desolate lie your farmlands.

Fruitfulness, your French name,
yet sterile is infrastructural development,
so frigidity reigns instead of blossom.

Reproduction, your Portuguese name,
yet your reign is repressive
and your children stampeded in commotion.

Industry, your English name,
but the ship of industry grounded,
'cause corruption and ineptitude ride with impunity.

Conducive atmosphere, your native name,
comfortable landscape and jungles everywhere,
yet inhabitable due to ethnic conflicts and wars.

Accountability, your surname,
but stunted by profiteering and praise singing
as sycophants tread the corridors of power.

Oh, the femur-shaped ebony beauty!
Who sucked your breasts dry?
No, No, not your colonial husbands!

My beloved sweetheart, now pale and sickly,
please rid your fingers of corruption
and see your beauty glitter like diamonds.

Today of Yesterday

At times like today,
one's love is remembered.
For the grace God showered on us,
in spite of our weaknesses,
it's worthwhile to thank Him,
for His wonderful love and gift of life.
Hence I rejoice with you
on your special day, today,
the today of the yesterday.

I rejoice with you
'cause when your light is precariously low,
God makes it glow and shine
like the day God created light.

I rejoice with you
'cause God lifts you up
when you're down, sinking,
like Jesus salvaged Peter.

I rejoice with you
when you're at the mountaintop
afraid of falling
'cause God gives you protection.

I rejoice with you,
'cause today is your birthday,
the today of yesterday.
I wish you many more blissful years.

Guess Who Comes for Dinner

We hear of your prowess
in nearby and distant suburbs,
but we never invited you for breakfast
because we're too greedy.

The jackboot of profiteers
trampled you to pulp
as slaps and spittle washed your face,
spit down from the selfish elite.

The energetic youthfulness
raped you to coma,
and you're dumped as trash
to die from neglect.

You survived the brutality
'cause you're destined to live.
Unwillingly, we invited you for dinner
by divine intervention.

Rather than allow you to eat,
you were sent to the kitchen
and when you emerged,
your meal was more palatable.

Democracy, the octopus of this generation,
your tentacles exude blissfulness.
Please, extend your stay with us
till death do we part.

The Cult

Bed fellows of bad fellows,
ideologically diverse
but financially converged.
Strange romance in strange marriage—
assembly of phony and foxy characters.

Cramped together like packed sardines,
the dance is samba at noon,
but a dirge at night
full of ratty businesses
biting and soothing your feet the game,
being technocrats in deceit.

The will must create a way—
plunder, squander, and unaccountable
leadership of lawlessness the game,
national cake the booty.
Public funds escalate and peculate
under impunity and immunity

The people's mandate in ruins
and the dividends as bad as soured grapes,
politicians faceless and rugged,
thin and skinny yesterday
but plump and rotund cheeks today.
The honest are plenteous like snake faeces,
but the fraudulent as scarce as the air,
yet ever stay put like glue, never willing to exit.

The Worm

Oh, Corruption, you are a cankerworm
created by the act of man.
Though highly reproductive,
you breed only one offspring, darkness,
that depletes our national leaves and trees.

Oh, Truth, you are so beautiful!
Though many say you're vile,
you're an unquenchable light.
Please come, come and light up our path
to disperse darkness into extinction
and digest our national forages.

Latent Potent

Just a few uttered words, or a few acts,
and adrenaline becomes high voltage
bustling through veins as gusty electrons.
She turns hard rock into red hot lava
and spews ash and molten rock,
so scotching the architect and neighbouring vegetation.

She makes the heart a pile-driver,
her footstep as a rumbling earthquake
pulling down everything on her path
since she's no respecter of persons.
She's a destructive force as of whirlwinds
who shreds the architect and neighbouring vegetation.

And at dawn tranquillity rears his head,
soberness, anguish, and regret the offspring.
Anger, you're a ferocious tiger
with eyes spitting fires.
This burns like Harmattan fire,
but it's stirred and nourished by fools.

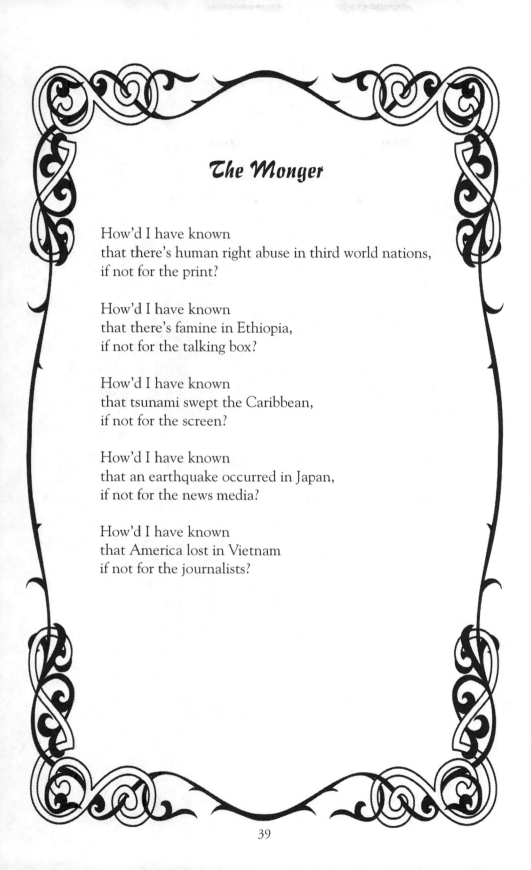

The Monger

How'd I have known
that there's human right abuse in third world nations,
if not for the print?

How'd I have known
that there's famine in Ethiopia,
if not for the talking box?

How'd I have known
that tsunami swept the Caribbean,
if not for the screen?

How'd I have known
that an earthquake occurred in Japan,
if not for the news media?

How'd I have known
that America lost in Vietnam
if not for the journalists?

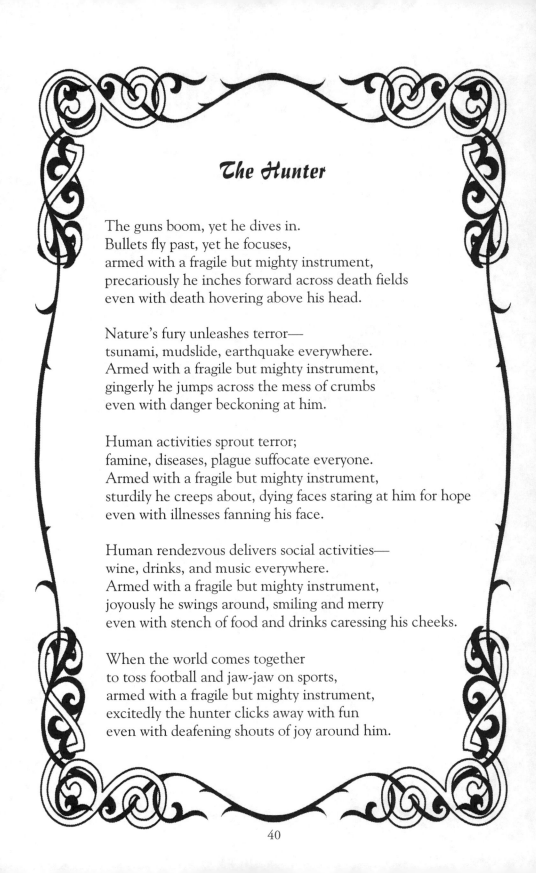

The Hunter

The guns boom, yet he dives in.
Bullets fly past, yet he focuses,
armed with a fragile but mighty instrument,
precariously he inches forward across death fields
even with death hovering above his head.

Nature's fury unleashes terror—
tsunami, mudslide, earthquake everywhere.
Armed with a fragile but mighty instrument,
gingerly he jumps across the mess of crumbs
even with danger beckoning at him.

Human activities sprout terror;
famine, diseases, plague suffocate everyone.
Armed with a fragile but mighty instrument,
sturdily he creeps about, dying faces staring at him for hope
even with illnesses fanning his face.

Human rendezvous delivers social activities—
wine, drinks, and music everywhere.
Armed with a fragile but mighty instrument,
joyously he swings around, smiling and merry
even with stench of food and drinks caressing his cheeks.

When the world comes together
to toss football and jaw-jaw on sports,
armed with a fragile but mighty instrument,
excitedly the hunter clicks away with fun
even with deafening shouts of joy around him.

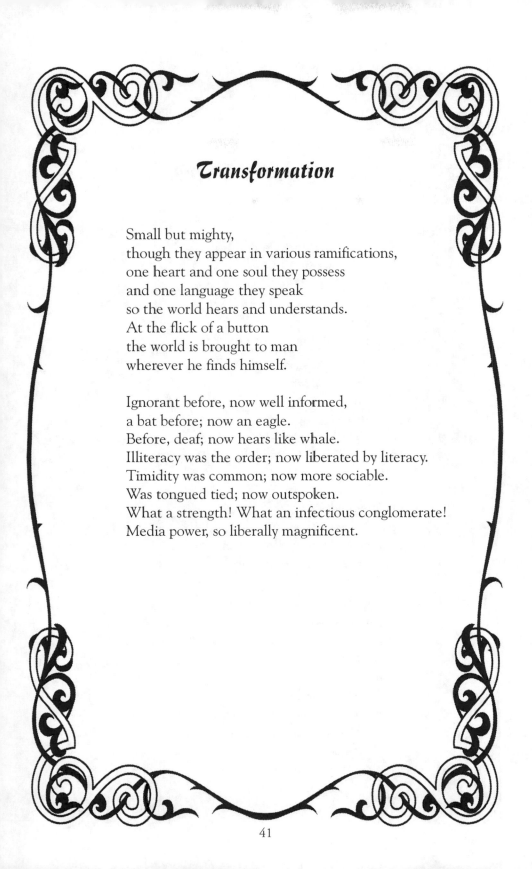

Transformation

Small but mighty,
though they appear in various ramifications,
one heart and one soul they possess
and one language they speak
so the world hears and understands.
At the flick of a button
the world is brought to man
wherever he finds himself.

Ignorant before, now well informed,
a bat before; now an eagle.
Before, deaf; now hears like whale.
Illiteracy was the order; now liberated by literacy.
Timidity was common; now more sociable.
Was tongued tied; now outspoken.
What a strength! What an infectious conglomerate!
Media power, so liberally magnificent.

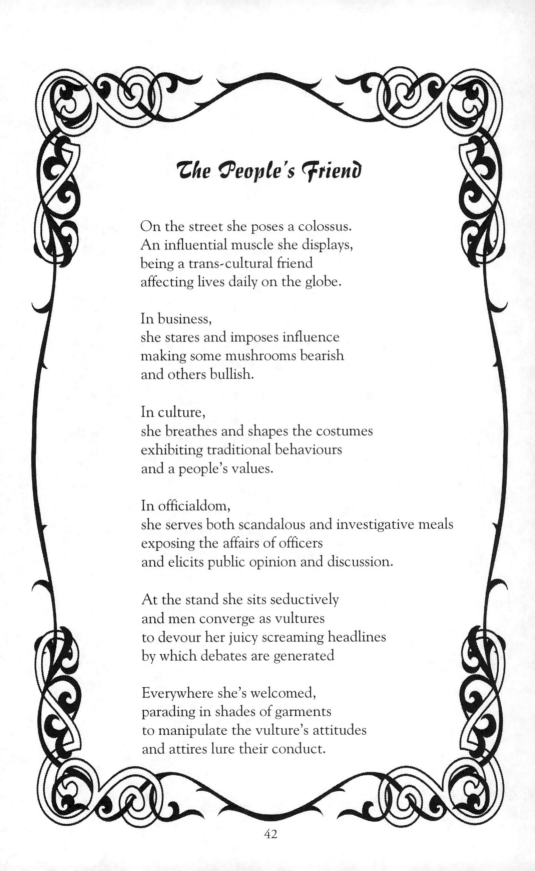

The People's Friend

On the street she poses a colossus.
An influential muscle she displays,
being a trans-cultural friend
affecting lives daily on the globe.

In business,
she stares and imposes influence
making some mushrooms bearish
and others bullish.

In culture,
she breathes and shapes the costumes
exhibiting traditional behaviours
and a people's values.

In officialdom,
she serves both scandalous and investigative meals
exposing the affairs of officers
and elicits public opinion and discussion.

At the stand she sits seductively
and men converge as vultures
to devour her juicy screaming headlines
by which debates are generated

Everywhere she's welcomed,
parading in shades of garments
to manipulate the vulture's attitudes
and attires lure their conduct.

Many faces she parades at will,
like the images of a multiple mirror—
advertisements, editorials, features, some faces,
interviews, sports, religion, others faces,
feedback, cartoons, and political matters, yet other faces.

She performs creditably well,
her availability, mobility, and in-depth coverage;
and being able to withstand the battering of the vultures
sometimes rendering her body freely
and most times at pittance,
I doff my cap, the powerful respected diva!

Good-bye Tomorrow

Oh, jet age development!
Walking with the elegance of kings,
what a beautiful perverted parade,
possessing ubiquitous omnipotence,
casting your shadow over the continents,
The great conqueror of our time.
Are you really not beautiful?

Oh, jet age development!
You're the harbinger of evil.
Your mechanised footsteps tremble the ground
as you grind high mountains into dust
and makes forests and streams vaporise like mirage,
leaving trails of patches like eczema-infested head.
Are you really beautiful?

Oh, jet age development!
The rivers have turn putrid with sheen,
the green leaves coloured as twilight,
as puffs from giant chimneys paint the sky dark,
thus hiking the price of breath.
Though ploughing and planting fertilisers,
the harvest is a bountiful mouthful.

Oh, jet age development!
You scientifically sculptured the globe,
but the environment limps,
for your fingers sketch death
as giant filth suffocates the flora and fauna.
Oh, mighty industrialisation, you've done good,
but the globe stinks with perspiration.

Sleep On

Man gave birth to science,
and science builds factories.
The factories produce beautiful things
yet defecate on the environment
and stigmatise flora and fauna.
These man must consume,
and man becomes bewitched.
If suffer not a witch to live,
then where is the tomorrow?
Oh, tomorrow is going!
And man will sleep to wake no more.
Man! Oh, man, wake up now!
For your snoring disturbs the peaceful scenery.
Wake up lest man become dinosaur.

Wait for Me!

Oh, precious time! Slow but determined,
please, wait for me until I'm ready.
But faster and faster she raced, slowly
slipping away with equanimity like twilight.
Time, oh, time! Slow but determined,
please, wait for me until I'm ready.
I wish I could hold you back and make amends.

Our Actions

Cough! Cough!! Cough!!!
But the air is pure and clean.
Gasp! Gasp!! Gasp!!!
I asphyxiate in plenteous air.
Oh! Oh! See! There!
Someone who ate rotten eggs just sneezed.
Run! Run, before we faint
for the stench is enormous,
like the cloud of a nuclear bomb,
and the trembling as violent as an earthquake—
but how can we escape
when the earth goes limp?